Healing Expressions

An Invitation to Freedom:
Healing & Awakening to Truth Through
Channeled Symbols, Divine Messages
& Intuitive Artistic Expressions

Michael Mollenhauer

with

Intuitive Artist

Jill Mollenhauer

Photos of Mike by Corey Reeves

Photos of Jill by Grant Jolly

Healing Expressions

We wish to welcome you to our book on healing and awakening. You have been drawn here for a reason, whether consciously or not, that there is more out "there" than what is traditionally taught. We congratulate you on this realization as being open is the key to healing. All healing comes from within and we all have the ability to heal ourselves. The physician, healer, surgeon, herbalist, dietician, etc. facilitates us in healing but the healing does not occur unless we choose it. We, in truth, are the healers.

"To open to and recognize that you do not know all the answers in your current state is the beginning of Healing. Knowing there is more than what you have been shown and seen is key to moving forward into claiming the essence of You. We ask you to take a moment to feel, to really feel with no thought, how each symbol affects you. And then ask, why? Why am I drawn to this symbol but I want to run away from that one? If you do this with purpose and intention, if you let yourself hear the answer, a new world awaits you as you open to the wonder of You! This is the True Healing."

"Michael has a beautiful insight to symbols and energy that is truly transformational. Anyone interested in channeling, healing or change will greatly benefit from his work."

~Weston Jolly,
Inspirational Speaker and Spiritual Channel

Table of Contents

Our Message of Love & Healing

Healing symbols are energetic keys that help open the flow of energy within us. Michael has been using these symbols quite effectively in his healing sessions since they were brought to him in meditation. These symbols, or energy maps, have specific purposes, some of which are physical or emotional healing, helping us to manifest our desires, assisting us in connecting spiritually, personal growth and much more. In addition to their use in energy healing work, many of the symbols are a great help as a focus point in meditation. Find a symbol you are drawn to, picture it in your mind, and meditate on it. You will be amazed at what you show yourself.

"Healing comes from within and we want you to know that there is nothing that you cannot create or do, if you choose it. As such, the choice to be out-of-balance, to be ill, is yours and yours alone. So is the choice to heal. Healing and illness can also be co-created experiences. There may be a family dynamic that wishes to experience a dramatic illness in the family, so that each may experience it in their own way. This is a collective choice. The same can be said for healing also. It can be an individual and a collective chosen experience. Whatever the case, the individual with the illness, must choose the healing, or not, as the experience is always free-will choice.

"Often in illness individuals choose someone to help facilitate with their recovery. This may be a physician, healer, friend, loved one, etc. and may include medicine, treatments, sound, symbols or other modalities. Symbols bring remembrance of, connection to, the Oneness of all things. They can trigger the universal memory within. As this remembrance is triggered healing can begin. This can be difficult for some of you to understand but this is no different than healing with herbs, medicine, sound, etc. Everything is energy. One energy is not better than another though some are more effective at bringing desired results in a certain area. As you look at, gaze upon, open to and feel a healing symbol, an energetic change takes place within your body, if you have chosen to open to the experience. This is energy working in the same manner as an herb or drug and with no adverse effects. We can and will assure you that all the answers are held within You. As you sit with these energy maps, these energetic keys, remembrance starts to flood in whether you are conscious of it or not.

"How can this be you say? We answer 'are you fully conscious of how aspirin is working on your headache in order to make it go away'? Ah, doctors and drug companies have told you so. We do not dispute this concerning aspirin but we would also say that much is not yet remembered concerning healing symbols. They are being brought back now specifically in this time and place. There are healings for areas in life that you cannot yet imagine. All is being brought back now—The Teachings. Soon all will be out there to be remembered. These symbols will help create openings, which will pave the way for what is to come.

"We encourage you to sit with any of the symbols you are drawn to. Feel what comes up and we encourage you to journal on it. Just let your thoughts go where they take you. We encourage you in this to drop your mind. Go with what you feel, come from the heart. Do not worry about or judge what comes up—just be with it and let it flow. This is healing in and of itself. As you do this you are opening the remembrance of whom you really are, no longer blocking or protecting or holding onto false paradigms that have been drilled into you.

"We encourage you to make this a part of your daily practice, if you so desire. Just set an intent, such as "opening your heart" and then sit with the symbol or symbols you are drawn to. Journal your thoughts and watch how your thoughts, feelings and actions change after a few days, a week, a month. We assure you that if you are open and desire change, you will be most pleased in what shows itself to you."

These healing symbols can also be used in much the same way as Reiki and other similar symbols. They can be used to heal yourself or others and the healings can be done hands-on or remotely. Picture the symbol, the symbol's name and/or the channeling in your mind and focus your energy, your intent on the healing. Focus on staying as open and clear as possible, making yourself a clear, clean conduit. If thoughts come up, do not worry on it, just watch them and let them drop if you can. Once you open the channel of healing, random thoughts will not negatively affect the flow unless your thoughts are ones of attachment or judgment. Attachments and judgments lessen and/or shut down the flow within us. Not only does this affect our ability to heal but also negatively affects our ability to manifest what we desire.

It is our desire that the Healing Expressions, contained on these pages, will bring you at least some of the joy, opening and healing that they have brought us. It is our greatest desire for all to discover the incredible, omnipotent soul within us all.

Namaste, Michael & Jill

Note: Healing symbols & channeled messages by Michael Mollenhauer (all paragraphs in quotes are channeled)
Painted expressions of the healing symbols & back cover channeling by Jill Mollenhauer

Balance/Spiritual Alignment, Integration

"Aligning and integrating your energies is most encouraged. Open yourself to the flow and align in the integration of creation. Be fully engaged and allow yourself to participate in all the wonders available to you. By your choice to open, align and integrate all becomes possible."

Balance/Spiritual Alignment, Integration

Releasing Pain

"Pain is nothing more than energy that is locked within. By giving credence to that which, in truth, is illusionary, it becomes 'real'. Opening to and embracing all that shows itself without choosing to attach creates a natural healing flow.

"Can you go within to see the source of your pain? With this choice to see it for what it truly is, all may be healed. Only by choice, free-will choice, does pain manifest. We encourage you to look within, into all your choices and see that which you have manifested as 'pain'. What is different about it from that which you proclaim as joy? Is it perception or truth? Is it opened or closed?

"All is offered to you in your choice to participate. How you choose, how you create is up to you. Know that in an instant you can shatter the illusion of a light side or dark side. There just Is. Will you allow yourself to be with what is, knowing that We are the essence of all? Can you look past any perceived pain and into the truth, as we are all One for now and forever? Be that for You are It."

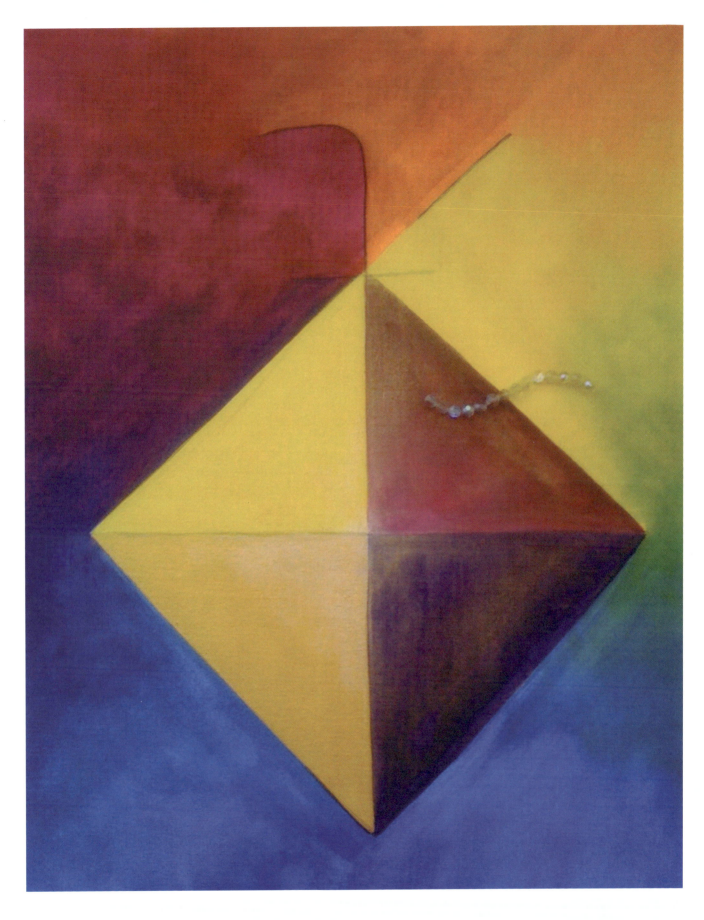

Releasing Pain

Oneness

"It is important to know that you are never alone, for how could you be when you are One with All That Is? Everything affects everything else—there is no separation. Rest assured that you can feel all if you choose and that you are truly felt everywhere. There is nothing that you cannot create as it is up to you and your choice to make. With but a choice you can drop any drama you have created and once again reside in the Love, the Wholeness and the Oneness that is Truly and Divinely You."

Oneness

Healing the Creator Within:
Healing the Root & Sacral Chakras, the Chakras of Creation

"Your power to create is beyond measure, what is it that you desire? Will you allow yourself to be the supremely powerful creator that is Divinely you? Or will you continue to limit yourself in the illusion that you are weak and a victim? We can assure you that you are not, for you are capable of creating all that you desire. Will you allow yourself to step out, open up and let the flow of creation run through you as you create and manifest that which you truly desire? The choice is yours. We encourage you to consider greatness for this is the essence of who you are."

Healing the Creator Within

Love

"Will you allow yourself to participate with the Source energy that drives the universe and is the basis of all creation? Will you come and play in the essence of who you are? We encourage you to participate in this remembrance of all that is you, for this is who you truly are and by connecting with this Source within you will light the world."

Love

Connect to Source

"Look within, look within, look within. For there you will find us. You need not go to any special place for we are always and ever with you. We await your desire, your wish to connect with us, who you really are.

"Do not worry about appearance or places or the state you are in and you are given to know what we mean. For there is no one that we are not a part of and none from which we would shy.

"So open your heart and ask for us and we will be here to talk with you. Yes talk, for there is no special requirement needed to do that which we most lovingly and happily do with all. Open, ask and in a quiet state you will hear us. Trust your heart in knowing we offer nothing but loving support. The paradigms held by so many are just that and nothing more. We are here to do nothing but offer love, encouragement and guidance. Look within, we are here."

Connect to Source

Passion/Wealth/Abundance/Empowerment

"When you engage in your passion, when you pursue that which truly excites you and moves you to tears, all will come to you. For when you are participating in that which you came here to do, you are open to all of Our wonders. You are a powerful being—your beautiful power to create fueled by your passion. Do you choose to live in the wealth and abundance that is so easily available to you? This is well within all of your abilities to manifest. There are no limitations except those that may be chosen by each one of you. Do you choose to fly or to tie yourselves down? This is your choice alone but realize that there are no constraints, nothing to hold you back from creating your dreams. We encourage you to fly on the wings of your inspiration."

Passion/Wealth/Abundance/Empowerment

Fire/Burning Away

"Do you feel the urge, the need, the desire to open yourself to new possibilities? Do you desire to drop that which hinders you, obstructs you, from connecting with that which you really want, that which truly moves you?

"If this is so, then give yourself permission to burn away, to melt away all the unwanted feelings, the emotional baggage that you have chosen to carry with you. Yes, that you have freely chosen to carry as yours. We ask you—does it serve you to be stuck, unable to go forward with that which you desire because of some fear, regret, sadness or anger that you have chosen to carry and, in addition, may not even be your worry, fear, regret or anger—but an emotion you have chosen to pick up as your own?

"We encourage you to sit quietly and truly feel what is within you, how you feel about certain situations that are predominant in your life. As you feel, truly feeling and most importantly not thinking, what shows itself to you? Take note and if you so choose, give yourself permission to drop these weights, these blocks that you have been carrying for they do not serve you or anyone else!

"Feel the fire of our love burning away the stranglehold of these locked-up emotions. Feel your fears and anger melt away opening you to infinite possibilities. What is not possible when you are open? The world is your playground to create all that you desire.

"So in your choice, we offer our healing love to dissolve any unwanted bonds and blockages. Let the light of our love free you so that you may burst forth in your magnificence!"

Fire/Burning Away

God Essence

"When you are centered and aware you will feel Us everywhere for we are imbued in all things. We are the essence of all. So why do so many feel the need to judge what is right and what is wrong as if We are only within those things which you have chosen to describe as 'good'.

"In truth We are in everything and in all experiences. And experiences and contrasts are why you are here. So We encourage you to find your preferences but to also refrain from labeling everything you see. Experience all you see, be one with it and in doing this, without judgment or attachment, you will connect with Us in each moment.

"This is your choice—to connect with Us in all things or to separate yourself as you judge and attach. By all means if the misery this brings is what you desire, then continue to go forth in this vein. But if Oneness, Love and Peace Within is your choice, then see Us everywhere you look, for indeed We are nowhere else."

God Essence

Karma/The Wheel/Rebirth

"You have chosen to come here for a specific purpose or purposes and this has created scenarios and situations to facilitate these lessons, these experiences you have chosen to create. Will you let yourself participate in these experiences knowing that you can, by your choice, create something different at any moment you choose? You are unlimited in all that you can create and We encourage you to reach for the stars if this is your desire. You are only stuck in any given situation or circumstance if this is what you choose. Realize that you can have whatever it is that you desire, irrespective of why or why not you have come. Should you choose to participate in your Divine expression then all the wonders of this plane will flow to you."

Karma/The Wheel/Rebirth

Energy Flow

"Flowing energy is the basis of good health and desired creations. When energy becomes blocked or stuck this flow of health and creation ceases. Opening to the flow is the essence of healing and creating."

Energy Flow

Fragmentation

"Are you feeling lost or scattered? Do you feel disjointed and all alone? If so, We would say that it is through your choice and your choice only. And with a new choice, the days of separation, the days of timeless wandering are over.

"By choosing to connect within to Us, to whom you really are, you will once again feel in your natural state of Wholeness, Oneness. We encourage all to be who they truly are, no longer living in the illusion of separation."

Fragmentation

Celestial Energy

"Does your heart sing? Can you feel the lightness? Do you feel like you can hop from star to star all the way to Heaven? Do you feel so expansive that there is no end in sight?

"If so, then you are tapped into the universal loving energy available to all. Breathe deeply and fill your lungs, your body, with Light. As you do you will find that there is nowhere that you cannot go. With but a breath you are limitless and the cosmos is your playground.

"So We encourage you to fill yourself with Light and Love as often as you desire. There is no limit to how much you can take for We are also limitless. Breathe, be still, and join Us whenever your heart should call. We are always here waiting."

Celestial Energy

Divine Mother

"When you feel lost and alone know that I am with you. Forever and always you are wrapped in my embrace. Only by choice can you not feel my love. So I ask you lovingly, if you desire to be One with Me, the purest of loves, then allow yourself to open and let Me in. As you open to my love, you will feel love begin to permeate throughout your being. This is the feeling of being One, of being Love, of being Loved. It is your natural state.

"So if this is your choice, open your heart and let my love, our love, come pouring in. In Truth it is already there, the pouring in is your remembrance of who you are. Open and be One with Us and all the worlds are yours."

Divine Mother

Strength/Power

"You are not limited in any way. The power you possess, the power you can call upon, is the power of all creation. Do you choose to feel small? If so, know that this is just a choice. Open yourself and call us within, filling you with the strength to do whatever it is you desire. We are here for you now and always. Do you choose to feel the strength within, the power that is most naturally you?"

Strength/Power

Oscillation/Vibrational Frequencies

"Everything is energy. We create change by changing the frequencies of the energies. To change frequencies, how the energy is conducted must change. Do you wish to expand in this your life? Then we encourage you to expand outwardly, opening to the new vibrations. As you open, inviting in the higher vibrations, you will find your creations being more of what you desire. You will also find your ability to manifest will increase in perceived speed. This is most beautiful and encouraged in your choice to create 'something more'.

"You need not open if this is not your desire for this is but a choice. If you so choose, you can shut down, limiting the vibrational frequencies you generate. In this choice you will find yourself creating things that might not be described as 'for your highest good'. But you may, by choice, open and ramp up the frequencies to create that which may be described as 'greater' or more 'desired'.

"We honor all your choices and this is why you can create from one end of the spectrum to the other. There are no rules and there are no limitations in this. The choice of what to create is yours and yours alone and all choices are honored equally by Us.

"But should you desire to create that which is Divinely You, if you desire to create outside the illusion of Maya, then We ask you to open and become a crystal clear conduit of energy. As you do, your thoughts, your desires, will be sent out as frequencies of the highest order, highest vibrations. As you do this, as you tap into this, who you really are, your thoughts, your creations, will speed to you in the most magnificent of manifestations.

"Opening to Truth, free of judgment and attachment, allows you to be this crystal clear vessel of manifestation. In doing this, in choosing this to the highest degree, you are stepping into your omnipotence. Do you understand what We are offering you? What We have always offered you? Will you allow yourself to be the Seat of Creation? The choice is yours, the Gift is Ours."

Oscillation/Vibrational Frequencies

Acknowledgment/Acceptance

"Acknowledging, accepting the Truth can be and is most scary for so many. Why is this so? We would think that learning, remembering your Divine nature would be cause for the utmost joy and excitement. Instead so many have chosen to cut themselves off from the Truth so that they may stay locked into the false paradigms that they have chosen to follow.

"Do you ever wonder at all the fear that you have all chosen to create on this plane? In doing so you have created great separation from that which is you. Do you understand? We think only partially, if at all.

"You are such magnificent Beings, truly Us in the body. So we ask, how can you be afraid of who you are? Does it not seem incongruous that you are afraid of being great, nay magnificent, but you clutch to limitations like they are the lifeblood of existence. Such interesting choices.

"Now is the time to look within and find Truth. It is time to look within and accept and acknowledge the Truth. In the doing so will you accept your Omnipotence? We certainly hope so. For there is no reason, other than the desire to experience pain, why you would choose to limit yourself in false belief. The choice to exist in the limited is not encouraged. It is not wrong for it is but a choice and you all have freewill choice. This is our greatest gift to you—one of absolute, unconditional Love. As you open and remember this will become clear to you.

"So, in our encouragement, will you allow yourself to fully accept and be That Which You Are in Truth? In this choice, all, all is yours. In the acknowledgment, in the acceptance, in the choosing, you once again become One with Us, One with All That Is. In truth you have never been aught but this, but this acceptance and choosing brings your total consciousness into the fold.

"All is changing, all is being sped up on this your place of chosen existence for now. If you desire to remain here, to live out your chosen time here in joy, peace, fulfillment and love, then we strongly encourage you of the most emphatic nature to accept and acknowledge Who You Are. In the doing so, It is Done. In the choice to remain blind, to remain separate, you will find that it will become grossly uncomfortable to remain Here and many will determine that it is time to depart—choices all choices.

"We offer you the most magnificent of rewards in your choice to be Divinely You. Will you accept, will you even acknowledge this Our gift to you? We hope so; We truly hope so. In all cases you are showered in our love always. The choice to grow in this rain of Love will always and forever be your choice."

Acknowledgment/Acceptance

Genesis/Exploding the Paradigms

"So where does creation begin? Is this something that happens 'out there' somewhere? Or perhaps is this something that germinates within you? We acknowledge that you know the answer within—will you allow yourself to go there?

"How can anything start without when you are One with All? There is no separation. Please know that you are the Creator of all that occurs in your world and more. We assure you that this is True. As the seed of desire springs to thought, waves of creation are set into motion. As you allow yourself to open to this desire of your creation, the waves build. As you completely open to your creation, the waves burst forth and bloom into manifestation. This, we assure you, happens with all your thoughts and desires. But in order to create fully on this plane, it takes more than just desire. It is important to look within to see if you are sending out clear messages on what it is you desire. And are you open to receive that which you say you desire to create? We can assure you that there is not always alignment here and this is a major cause of your 'supposed' desired creations not coming into manifestation.

"In order to create, there must be alignment within. Are you clear in your desire, will you allow yourself and are you fully open, to receive it? Can you let the desire out without attachment to when it will manifest? We assure you that the process of creation is really quite simple and only through your choice to be confused has it become 'hard'. In your choice to choose to open, to engage and to just be, all will be created as per your desires.

"As all was created in the beginning, so can you create now. For you are the creators of your world. Do you understand this? You are not a victim of anything for all you have manifested, all that has occurred, is the result of your creation. Know this as Truth.

"So you ask us, 'how could I have created this most dramatic disease? I would never want that.' We say, is that so? Then why are you so conflicted within? Why do you not wish to be in alignment and truth? Your creations mirror your inward state of being. If you are living in chaos, if you do not want to see for fear of some perceived pain or hurt, how can you create that which you say you desire? We say you cannot. In your choice to align, to be free of judgment and attachment, your creations, your manifestations, will be most magnificent and Divine.

"So to create beauty, become the beauty that you are. Be assured that all of you, without exception, are of Us. No matter what your choice of creation here, in your choice to return Home, you will once again realize the Divinity that is You, is Us.

"So what do you choose to create? The choice is yours, the possibilities are endless. With your choice it is just as easy to create that which you truly desire as it is to create the chaos that so many have chosen to immerse themselves in. With your choice, we encourage you to create the Divinity that is You."

Genesis/Exploding the Paradigms

The Heart Chakra: The Flow, The Wheel of Love

"Energy flows throughout your body, this vessel you have chosen in order to experience this plane of existence. The openness, the unrestrictedness, of the flow determines your physical, mental and spiritual health. When the flow of energy is constricted, you are not able to function at your full capacity.

"In truth this is no different from the problems a car experiences when you constrict the flow of gasoline. It does not matter where the constriction is the effect is the same, poor performance. We would say that the same can be said of your bodies. These bodies, these vessels, these shells, you inhabit will not run properly if the energy within is constricted. If you desire to experience the highest of performances in this your chosen experience, then We encourage you to open to the flow.

"As you open fully to the flow, through breath, through the honoring of this body that you have chosen to inhabit, your awareness will intensify. You will remember who you are. If this sounds desirous, then we encourage you to open fully in order to experience the most magnificent of creations—life on this plane while still being fully connected to whom you really are.

"Choosing to forget You, Us, is just a choice and one that We always honor but it is not a necessary choice. You can choose to be One with Us always. The choice to be connected as One is not limited to only those in 'good' health. This is available to everyone in any moment, with the choice to reconnect with Us.

"In your body there are many energy centers, large and small. The larger ones you call chakras. We would say that the 'command' center of these chakras is your heart chakra. For if your heart is not open, how can you receive Us? How can you love yourself or anyone for that matter if this center is closed down? This spinning wheel of Love within you is Us. Will you allow yourself to connect with it, with Us? In the choice to do so you can never be separate for We are always as One.

"So We encourage you to open your heart, to say yes to Us, to Love. When you are connected with Us you will find that there is no need for fear, hate, separation, loneliness, greed, judgment or attachment. In connection you have it all so there is nothing to grasp for or to hold onto in fear of loss. When you see yourself as whole you will remember that this is your natural state. In this natural omnipotent state your ability to create is limitless. Your ability to love is limitless. You will remember the ability to just Be. In this moment you are It and there is no more searching or protecting.

"Will you allow yourself, will you invite yourself, to connect with your Heart Center, the place of union for You and Us. In your choosing you will once again be One with the limitless expression that is You."

The Heart Chakra: The Flow, The Wheel of Love

Ascension

"Do you choose to return Home? This can be done at anytime with just a choice. Please know that it is not necessary to interrupt your experience here on this plane. The choice is one of remembrance, the choice to remember all that you are and will always be. Do you choose to participate in this energy of your true natural state or do you choose to stay disconnected, to remain separate from that which you truly are?

"We offer this choice to you now and always. We offer the encouragement that the experiences you are playing with here can be of the most fun and interesting types. They only need be dramatic if this is your choice. It always comes back to your choice. So ask yourself now—what is it that I desire—to be in the flow of never-ending unconditional love or in the separate state of illusion? We honor your choices always and none are or could be considered 'wrong'. The choice is yours—what will you choose? We bow to you in honor of your choice and to all that you are."

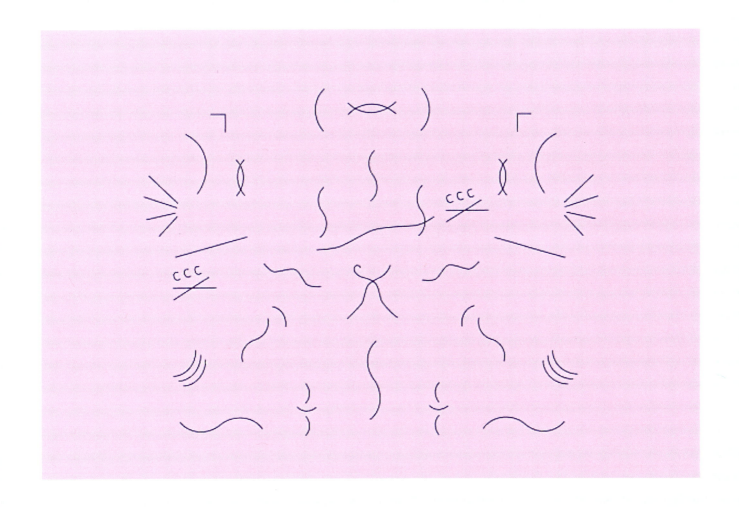

Ascension

The Divine Heart

"From whence does all love and knowledge flow? What is the wellspring of all that is? Is it ever flowing and available to all? Most assuredly yes—all one need do is open and invite Us in. Will you allow yourself to truly open and to invite Us in without fear or conditions that close the gate? We are always with you. To be fully connected We encourage you to open to that place of peace and just Be."

The Divine Heart

Freewill Choice

"Your choice to choose your experiences, what you desire, whatever it is you desire, is Our gift to you, to Us. Allowing you to be the creator, the designer of your experience, is the greatest gift We can give you. We honor you in all of your choices whether or not you choose to label them dark or light, right or wrong. Even when these labels are not verbalized most of you carry the energy of these judgments of being good or bad. We suggest that you drop the carrying of these judgments for they block that which you wish to create. There is no right or wrong just creation. It is for all of you to decide what it is you desire to create, what is it that brings you joy or what is it that brings pain, if this is what you wish to experience.

"We encourage you to feel the power within freewill choice. Feel the power within this choice. So many of you have chosen to be deadened to this power inherent in this gift. We wish to enlighten you to the fact that when you open and align yourself to that which you desire, when you make your freewill choice, the power unleashed dwarfs any of your atomic energies. For this is the power of creation and when creation is unleashed with no constraints nothing can stop the power that has been loosed. So We ask you to take a moment to feel, to be with the power you wield. How can you be anything other than omnipotent in your truest of states? Be assured what We say is true and correct. See the power within, know the power within, and you can easily create your greatest and wildest of dreams."

Freewill Choice

Bodily Purification: Opening the Channels to Health

"Energy flowing freely is the key to good health. Purifying the body's energies, removing vibrational blocks, opens the pathways, the channels, so that energy flows easily and naturally throughout the body. When the energies run evenly and rhythmically throughout you, health manifests—which is your natural state.

"Focus on your desired state for we encourage you to 'see' your healthy body brimming with vitality. See this no matter how you are feeling. Focus on this symbol of health and feel these forces within you as all flows together synergistically. Hear it, feel it, know it. As you do the energies within your body will balance. When they balance, health comes. In your choice to do this, in your choice to choose to open and choose health, you can exist in this most beautiful of states regardless of how you feel now or have felt historically. Anything can be manifested with but a choice. What do you choose?"

Bodily Purification

Cellular Rebirth: Tuning to Source Frequency

"So you once again wish to vibrate at your more natural state? Is this not so? We feel you pulling back from the 'out-of-balance' scenarios you have created. Have you engaged, explored and immersed yourself for long enough in the energies that are not naturally You or Us? Do you feel the strong desire to reconnect with the highest of frequencies but you are not sure how? Then take a moment to Breathe—always return to Breath, for this Life Force Is of Us. Reconnect to Us through Breath. Draw Us in and feel Us, Be Us. How is this you say? How could it not be for you are Us. You have only forgotten.

"So take a moment to remember if this pleases you. Find a quiet state and breathe, connecting more deeply with Us in each breath. Focus upon, gaze upon, dive into, this beautiful map of Remembrance. It is all here—the entire Creation Process. We realize it will take you a moment or two or more to remember but We assure you that if you choose to open, truly open, you will feel this in a most profound way. Your true essence will remember though there will be in most cases a reacclimation period for your shell—even if you decide to open fully and immerse yourself in remembrance of you.

"So do you wish to begin again anew? Do you wish to be rebirthed, reborn, not as an infant but as the fully illumed soul and body you are in Truth? If so, if yes, then take Our gift of Love, of Remembrance, of Creation, and pull it into your heart and soul—into every crevice of your Being. Once again you are, We are, One."

Cellular Rebirth: Tuning to Source Frequency

"Everything is energy and energy has it own rhythm, signature. Energy is light. By combining energies, weaving energies, magnificent new creations occur. The same holds true for healing. By weaving together energies in a synergistic play, untold possibilities unfold. This weaving creates 'something more'. Experience the wonder, the power of creation, and if you allow yourself to play along, the magnitude of your creations will grow and no doubt astound you."

Healing Clusters

Working with groups of symbols is a very powerful way to create the healing, change or manifestation that you desire. When properly combined the symbols, just like the ingredients in a recipe, create something greater than the sum of their parts. Putting together clusters, groups of symbols, whose energies flow together and compliment one another, can help create profound change.

We encourage you to sit with these clusters as you would with individual symbols. Set an intention before starting, breathe, and open to what shows itself. It can also be very effective to journal any thoughts that arise. As you do the energies released trigger the healing and/or manifestation to begin.

Passionately Creating Your Desires

"What is it that you truly desire? What is it that you desire and will allow yourself to have? You are wondering—that is a strange question-but We assure you it is not. We find that more often than not there is not alignment between the stated desire and being open to receive it.

"You say you would like to create a sizable income but there is a part of you that feels unworthy to receive it. We can assure you that this will prevent the manifestation from occurring. If you find yourself unable to create what you 'think' you desire, then we encourage you to look at both the desire and your openness to receive it. Go within and 'feel', really 'feel', if this is something you desire. We encourage you to remember that thinking and feeling are not the same. Say your stated desire is for a red truck and this is something you tell everyone. If this is in truth, then you will be able to feel the passion and desire burning within. If you cannot feel it, then your stated desire is not in truth and/or is a weak or blocked desire. If you can feel this desire passionately but you are not manifesting it, then We ask you to look within to see if you feel worthy to receive it. Feel this as perhaps you feel unworthy to receive it because you have been told this your entire life.

"Whatever the case, look deeply at this unworthiness piece. Or perhaps it is fear that keeps what your desire away? Look deeply to see why and then by your choice you may drop it. Once this block, this energy holding you back, is dropped, you are open to manifest your desire.

"So We invite you to sit with these three symbols and feel them begin to open you. What passions do you feel? Do you feel the passion of your stated desire or another passion you have not allowed yourself to see? Gaze at the symbols and then shut your eyes and feel within—what is it you feel—passion or blocks? Continue until you find your passion and you have cleared an energetic pathway to receive it. Then know that it is yours. And in the knowing it is done. Let it go and do not attach to when, how, what, where, etc, just know that it is on the way and you will be guided appropriately so that your desire will manifest. Open, feel and let it go. Do this for whatever you desire and watch your manifestations bloom."

Discovering Your Life's Divine Purpose

"Are you passionate in your life about all that you do? Do you feel as though you cannot wait to wake in the morning so that you can pursue your passion? Or do you feel as though you have to be dynamited out of bed so that you may go once more to your chosen job, chosen profession?

"When you are connected with why you came Here, when you know what it is you love to do, when passion pours out of you just thinking about it, then you are engaged in your Divine Life's Purpose.

"All have a chosen Divine Purpose but so many choose not to engage in it. Why is that you wonder? We say because so many of you have chosen to be locked by your judgments, attachments and fears. You have chosen to become paralyzed by what others might think, by your judgments of whether something is good enough for you or not, even if it gives you the greatest pleasure imaginable. Some are just plain afraid to look at what they truly desire.

"Take a moment to look within and see. What makes your heart pound and brings tears to your eyes at the mere thought of doing? What moves you to tears? Worry not about how or why or what or when. Feel it and when you find it, if you should choose to engage in this your Divine Purpose, all is yours. There is nothing you cannot conquer for you are engaged in doing what you have come here to do.

"So sit with these symbols and let your mind flow to that place that excites you, moves you, beyond all else. This is your Divine Creation. We encourage you to leap in and engage—to Have Fun! For when you are doing what it is you came to do, it is the most fun. No longer will you go to work but to Play. And play of the most magnificent kind. We salute you in your choice to look within, to look deeper, to search and find that place you have chosen to keep hidden. This is You—grab it and run and play for the world, this world, is Yours!"

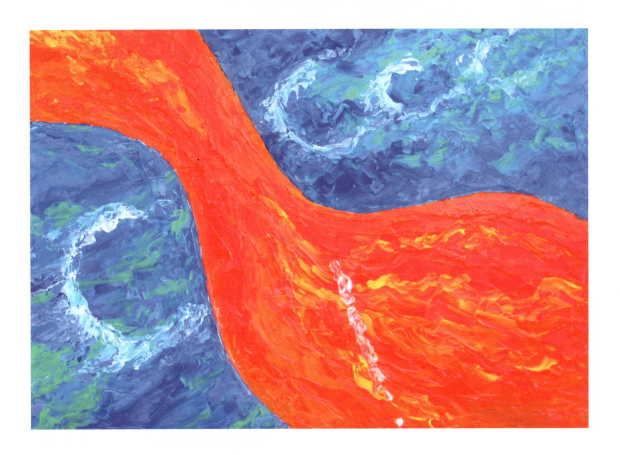

Healing/Optimum Health

"Opening to the flow is opening to health. Returning your body, your shell you have chosen for this existence, to its fully functioning ability, through free-will choice, is the path to Divine Health. Do you choose to drop these paradigms of unbalanced states? Do you choose to align the flow of energies within? If this is your choice, and it is most encouraged if you desire to exist in the highest of states, then We ask you to open and to be aware of where the flow is blocked within you. We assure you that you all can feel it, if you so choose.

"Find a quiet place and still your mind. Feel the flow of Us within you. Can you feel where all flows freely and where you are shut down and the energies are blocked? We assure you that you can do this quite easily if you will but allow it. In your quiet state go to those places that feel stagnant and feel the cause behind the stagnation. Ask if you so desire and We will gladly answer you. If you remain open We assure you that you will hear, see, feel or know the answer. Then just be with it. It may make sense to you or it may not—this does not matter. What matters, the crux, is to get the energies aligned and flowing once more.

"We offer you these symbols, these maps, in remembrance of You. By sitting with them, focusing on them, meditating with them, pathways will open within you. Your higher self will remember and this will be transmitted to your body. In the doing so the Healing begins. This series, this batch, this cluster, of Healing symbols is designed to reopen the flow and to promote health and vitality within—to promote the most beautiful state of Being within the confines of a body. This is and there is no judgment on how your body should be. Perhaps it is not functioning at its highest efficiency because you have chosen to show yourself something, to experience a different state. To this We say, please move forward in this if this is your chosen desire. But if you have seen enough or just wish to create something different, We offer this gift of Love, of Healing, of Remembrance. Play with this Love if you so desire and once again feel the finely tuned machine that you have chosen to inhabit. In all cases and in all choices We are here with you always. The choice to connect is at all times yours but be not mistaken We are always with you and within you for We are You. How could We be anyplace else?

"So take a moment and let yourself remember. We encourage you not to judge, question or attach. Just be with Us and Our offering of Love. May peace within and without be with you."

Rebuilding the Temple Within:
Aligning, Integrating the Spiritual with the Physical

"It is for you to know that there is no separation. All is One. In this you are wont to know that you have created, on this plane, separation everywhere and in everything. When in truth everything is intertwined. How could it not be for it is all of Us? Take a moment for this to process within you, for the ramifications, the changes available to you as you absorb and realize this basic truth, are great and profound to say the least.

"Spiritual and physical, physical and spiritual—are they different entities or one and the same? We ask you to look at the paragraph above if you do not know the answer. Everything is spiritual for this is indeed Us and We are also the basis of all that is physical here on this plane. So how do you separate any of this from Us? We can assure you that you do not.

"We encourage you to know that this time in this realm, this plane of existence, is an experience of both the spiritual and physical nature. No longer need you hide in one expression or the other in the fear that you may get hurt in participating in both. Now is the time of the Great Change, the Time of Bringing it All Together. The Age of Awareness, the Age of Oneness.

"If you desire the highest and most vibrant of experiences here, in this your bodily journey, then We encourage you to embrace it All. Absolutely realize, remember, the omnipotent, spiritual being that you are and thus, in this realization and knowing that you are this spiritual being having this physical, human experience, all can be enjoyed with wonder. Engage fully in knowing the spiritually magnificent being you are, playing this incredible part, role, of a physical manifestation. In your knowingness, in your remembrance, it becomes clear that you cannot get hurt. For how can you when you are Us? Play, play, play and realize each step is a spiritual experience while also realizing the physical playground you have chosen to visit.

"We ask you to enjoy all the wonders this plane offers you while remembering who you really are. With each breath watch your omnipotence flow through your body, your actions, your life here. Be at One with each breath, each moment and know that you have created the totality of this experience so that you may engage in all the wonders and contrasts available to you.

"Take a moment and a breath and feel yourself, really remember yourself. Do you just feel a physical body? Do you just feel your spiritual essence? We think not. Do you feel them both flowing together in a synergistic play? Do you see the doors opening all around you as this awareness permeates you? So beautiful. Be with the symbols, breathe them in and see and feel all that you are. You are unlimited, you are aware, you are One!"

Personal & Intention Symbols

Personal Symbols and Intention Symbols are tremendously effective in helping to manifest desires, assist in connecting spiritually, in personal growth, in healing and much more. Both types of symbols are precisely attuned to your energy to help create the specific change desired.

A Personal Symbol maps your energy and the energetic essence of why you are here. Many people are able to actually feel their energy coming off the page. Sitting and working with your Personal Symbol helps create openings to accelerate your growth.

Intention Symbols are specifically tailored to your energy to help you create whatever it is you desire. Working together we establish exactly what it is you desire to create. Once this desired intent is clearly ascertained I channel a symbol unique to you and your desired intent. I also am given (I channel) a message for you concerning your intent, your symbol and how best to use your symbol in helping you to create your desired manifestation.

Both symbols are very powerful energetic keys created to open the flow of energy within and without you, enabling the healing and/or manifestation to begin. If you desire to know more, please visit mikemollenhauer.com

"Mike, I just wanted you to know that since I received the intention symbols from you I have opened up and am painting again. And beyond that I feel a far greater opening happening within. The doors have cracked open to my passions and I am creating on a whole new level. I feel so much love knowing that you focused on my intention with me and I feel that every time I work with the symbol, which just opens me up more.

Thank you so much Mike for giving me such an incredible gift of love and intention! My world is filled with the passionate me again and I am so grateful for your assistance with this very precious opening."

Karen, Phoenix, Arizona

Healing with Symbols

Michael Mollenhauer is an intuitive energy healer, teacher and spiritual channel. By healing ourselves within, not only can we heal our bodies but also our relationships and life situations. Using symbols he has channeled along with his energetic and intuitive abilities Michael focuses on any physical or emotional areas that need attention enabling the healing to begin from within.

To learn more please visit mikemollenhauer.com

About the Painted Symbols

Jill Mollenhauer, Michael's sister and a San Diego based artist, has an uncanny ability to capture the energy intrinsic in Michael's symbols within her own works of art.

For more information regarding symbol paintings or reprints and to see more of Jill's work please visit jillmollenhauer.com.

Dedicated with much love and gratitude to our teacher & mentor, Weston Jolly.

Printed in the United States
151064LV00002B